4 minute
BIBLE STUDIES

Finding Hope After Divorce

DISCARD / ÉLIMINÉ

Kay Arthur

PRECEPT MINISTRIES INTERNATIONAL

WATERBROOK
P R E S S

FINDING HOPE AFTER DIVORCE
PUBLISHED BY WATERBROOK PRESS
12265 Oracle Boulevard, Suite 200
Colorado Springs, Colorado 80921

Trade Paperback ISBN 978-1-60142-558-4
eBook ISBN 978-1-60142-559-1

Published in the United States by WaterBrook Multnomah, an imprint of the Crown Publishing Group, a division of Random House LLC, New York, a Penguin Random House Company.

WATERBROOK and its deer colophon are registered trademarks of Random House LLC.

Printed in the United States of America
2014—First Edition

10 9 8 7 6 5 4 3 2 1

CONTENTS

HOW TO USE THIS STUDY

This small-group study is for people who are interested in learning for themselves more about what the Bible says on various subjects, but who have only limited time to meet together. It's ideal, for example, for a lunch group at work, an early morning men's group, a young mothers' group meeting in a home, a Sunday-school class, or even family devotions. (It's also ideal for small groups that typically have longer meeting times—such as evening groups or Saturday morning groups—but want to devote only a portion of their time together to actual study, while reserving the rest for prayer, fellowship, or other activities.)

This book is designed so that all the group's participants will complete each lesson's study activities *at the same time.* Discussing your insights drawn from what God says about the subject reveals exciting, life-impacting truths.

Although it's a group study, you'll need a facilitator to lead the study and keep the discussion moving. (This person's function is *not* that of a lecturer or teacher. However, when this book is used in a Sunday-school class or similar setting, the teacher should feel free to lead more directly and to bring in other insights in addition to those provided in each week's lesson.)

If *you* are your group's facilitator, the leader, here are some helpful points for making your job easier:

- Go through the lesson and mark the text before you lead the group. This will give you increased familiarity with the material and will enable you to facilitate the discussion with greater ease. It may be easier for you to lead the group through the instructions for marking the text, if you, as a leader, choose a specific color for each symbol you mark.

- As you lead the group, start at the beginning of the text and simply read it aloud in the order it appears in the lesson, including the "insight boxes," which appear throughout. Work through the lesson together, observing and discussing what you learn. As you read the Scripture verses, have the group say aloud the word they are marking in the text.

- The discussion questions are there simply to help you cover the material. As the class moves into the discussion, many times you will find that they will cover the questions on their own. Remember, the discussion questions are there to guide the group through the topic, not to squelch discussion.

- Remember how important it is for people to verbalize their answers and discoveries. This greatly strengthens their personal understanding of each week's lesson. Try to ensure that everyone has plenty of opportunity to contribute to each week's discussions.

- Keep the discussion moving. This may mean spending more time on some parts of the study than on others. If necessary, you should feel free to spread out a lesson over more than one session. However, remember that you don't want to slow the pace too much. It's much better to leave everyone wanting more than to have people dropping out because of declining interest.

- If the validity or accuracy of some of the answers seems questionable, you can gently and cheerfully remind the group to stay focused on the truth of the Scriptures. Your object is to learn what the Bible says, not to engage in human philosophy. Simply stick with the Scriptures and give God the opportunity to speak. His Word *is* truth (John 17:17)!

FINDING HOPE AFTER DIVORCE

I want a divorce." You may have heard it. You may have said it. Either way, the words speak of failure—and failure is hard to bear, hard to excuse, hard to accept, and hard to get over.

Some people say those words—"I want a divorce"—are more devastating than learning of a mate's death. Death brings marriage to an end; there's no recourse, no reversal. But in divorce, you both still live. And you have to live with that!

If the words came from your mate, then more than likely you feel faulted, rejected, scorned, cast away.

Questions flood your mind: *What am I going to do? How will I survive? Who will take care of me? What about the children? Whose side will they take? What will people think of me? What does God think of me?*

When you try to look ahead to the future, all you can see are more questions:

Am I doomed to be alone forever? Damaged goods?

Will God ever again use me in ministry, or will I always wear a scarlet D in Christian circles? What will people in the church think? How will they treat me?

And what about our friends? Whose friends will they be? Will aloneness define my life?

We could fill pages with question upon question—some rational, some irrational. Questions that keep you awake, that won't go away, that keep you wondering how you will ever get out of bed and do life in the morning.

So how can you get through this? Live with it?

First and foremost, you need to know that if you are a child of God, believe it or not, you are beloved of God. He says it over and over again in His book, the Bible.

And if you're not His child yet, then the reason you have this book in your hands is because God wants to lavish His love on you. He wants to call you *beloved,* even though you may feel there is nothing lovable about you.

Second, you need to know that divorce does not take God by surprise. Because God is God, because He is omniscient—all knowing—He knew your divorce was coming. And although He does not like divorce because of the pain and damage it brings to our lives, God knows that, because of the hardness of our hearts, some will choose the path of divorce.

However, with God, that's not the end. God describes Himself in the Bible as the divine Potter, the One who is able to reshape your life into a vessel of beauty. He'll put you back on His potter's wheel, rewet your clay with the water of His Word, and shape you into a man, a woman of praise, renown, and glory if you will become putty in His hands.

In Psalm 107:20, God offers to send His Word and heal us, to deliver us from our destructions if we will listen to what He says, believe Him, trust Him, obey Him. He is a redeemer, the God of all hope.

Having experienced personally the devastating effects of divorce and an immoral lifestyle, I can assure you that your life is not over. Damaged, yes, but not ruined if you will take God at His word and cling to Him.

The question is, are you willing to give it a try? I pray so.

Over the next six weeks you are going to learn much from God's Word and from those in your group who take God at His Word. God tells us two are better than one (Ecclesiastes 4:9), and though you've lost or are losing your mate, you are sure to find a sister, a brother to walk through this with you as take God's hand and follow His path.

Divorce hurts. Even if we pursued it, the death of a marriage just plain hurts. And you wonder, *Will I ever be whole again? Will these wounds ever heal?*

When a marriage is destroyed by divorce, you don't simply return to being who you were before you were married. God's Word tells us in marriage two become one flesh (Matthew 19:6). Divorce destroys that oneness, resulting not in two whole individuals but in one flesh torn in pieces, often leaving raw, tender wounds. Just the thought of your loss brings wincing pain. Consequently you may be tempted to ignore those wounds, to cover them up with something or someone— anyone!

But covering your wounds won't bring healing, and when wounds are not properly treated, they fester. Eventually infection will set in.

This, beloved of God, is why we must look to the Word of God for healing. And that is what we are going to do this first week. We'll look at some raw emotions, see how they are to be handled, and find hope for the rest of this day—and for all of your tomorrows.

OBSERVE

Leader: Read Jeremiah 17:14 and Psalm 107:19–21 aloud, slowly. Have the group say aloud and mark each key word or phrase as directed:

- *Underline every pronoun referring to **the person** and **the people**, including **me**, **I**, **my**, **they**, and **them**.*

JEREMIAH 17:14

Heal me, O LORD, and I will be healed; save me and I will be saved, for You are my praise.

PSALM 107:19–21

19 Then they cried out to the LORD in their trouble; He saved them out of their distresses.

20 He sent His word and healed them, and delivered them from their destructions.

21 Let them give thanks to the LORD for His lovingkindness, and for His wonders to the sons of men!

• *Mark every reference to **the Lord,** including the pronouns **You, He,** and **His**—with a triangle, like this:* △
As you read the text, it's helpful to have the group say the key words aloud as they mark them. This way everyone will be sure they are marking every occurrence of the word, including any synonymous words or phrases. Do this throughout the study.

DISCUSS

• What did you learn from marking *I* and *me* in Jeremiah 17:14?

• Why did you learn about the people— the *they* and *them*—in Psalm 107?

• What did you learn from marking the references to the Lord in both passages?

• According to Psalm 107, where does deliverance come from?

• Does that tell you anything? If so, what?

• What is your pain? Do you carry guilt because of a failed marriage? Or can you not forget or forgive the stinging words, the accusations? What do you most want to be healed from, saved from, delivered from?

Leader: Ask if someone would be brave enough to break the ice by sharing an answer to the preceding question. Give them a few moments. If no one shares, that is fine, as they may not yet feel comfortable with one another.

Leader: Now have the group read Jeremiah 17:14 aloud as a request to the Lord.

PSALM 88:1–9, 18

¹ O LORD, the God of my salvation, I have cried out by day and in the night before You.

² Let my prayer come before You; incline Your ear to my cry!

³ For my soul has had enough troubles, and my life has drawn near to Sheol.

⁴ I am reckoned among those who go down to the pit; I have become like a man without strength,

⁵ Forsaken among the dead, like the slain who lie in the grave, whom You remember no more, and they are cut off from Your hand.

OBSERVE

Leader: Read Psalm 88:1–9, 18 very slowly so that God's words might sink in. Have the group...

- *mark every reference to **the Lord**, including pronouns, with a triangle.*
- *underline every **I, my, me**.*

INSIGHT

Sheol is basically a reference to the grave, to death.

Selah is a word found in the Psalms that may indicate a pause, a crescendo, or a musical interlude. When you see it in a psalm, take it as a reminder to pause and consider what you just read.

Leader: Read through the verses again, slowly.

- *This time, have the group place a check mark like this ✓ over **any words or phrases that relate to them**, that describe how they feel.*

DISCUSS

• In what ways, if any, can you relate to the experience of the person speaking in these verses?

• Who is the psalmist talking to, and why?

• What does this tell you about the psalmist's beliefs about God?

• Does this shock you? Does it bring questions to your mind? If so, what are they?

⁶ You have put me in the lowest pit, in dark places, in the depths.

⁷ Your wrath has rested upon me, and You have afflicted me with all Your waves. Selah.

⁸ You have removed my acquaintances far from me; You have made me an object of loathing to them; I am shut up and cannot go out.

⁹ My eye has wasted away because of affliction; I have called upon You every day, O Lord; I have spread out my hands to You.…

¹⁸ You have removed lover and friend far from me; my acquaintances are in darkness.

INSIGHT

When you study the Old Testament, you encounter scripture after scripture that testifies to the sovereignty of God, to the fact that God rules supremely over all. In Deuteronomy 32:39 God says, "See now that I, I am He, and there is no god besides Me; it is I who put to death and give life. I have wounded and it is I who heal, and there is no one who can deliver from My hand."

The name of God that testifies to His sovereignty is *El Elyon,* which means "the Most High God." This name appears frequently in the book of Daniel. Nebuchadnezzar, the king of Babylon, after being greatly humbled by God, declared, "My reason returned to me, and I blessed the Most High and praised and honored Him who lives forever; for His dominion is an everlasting dominion, and His kingdom endures from generation to generation.... He does according to His will in the host of heaven and among the inhabitants of earth; and no one can ward off His hand or say to Him, 'What have you done?'" (Daniel 4:34–35).

Isaiah, led by God, recorded a prophecy written over one hundred years before the birth of Cyrus, a future king of the Medo-Persian Empire. In that prophecy he addressed that future monarch by name, once again confirming God's sovereignty: "Thus says the LORD to Cyrus His annointed..., 'I am the LORD, and there is no other; besides Me there is no God. I will gird you, though you have not known Me; that men may know from the rising to the setting of the sun that there is no one besides Me. I am the LORD, and there is no other, the One forming light and creating darkness, causing well-being and creating calamity; I am the LORD who does all these'" (45:1, 5–7).

When you understand that God is sovereign, you realize you are not in the hands of fate, another human being, the devil, or mother nature. No, it is Father God who holds you in His loving hands, and once you get to know Him and live accordingly, you'll experience a peace that can carry you through any and every circumstance of life—even divorce.

PSALM 6:1–10

¹ O LORD, do not rebuke me in Your anger, nor chasten me in Your wrath.

² Be gracious to me, O LORD, for I am pining away; heal me, O LORD, for my bones are dismayed.

³ And my soul is greatly dismayed; but You, O LORD—how long?

⁴ Return, O LORD, rescue my soul; save me because of Your lovingkindness.

⁵ For there is no mention of You in death; in Sheol who will give You thanks?

⁶ I am weary with my sighing; every

OBSERVE

David endured a great deal in his lifetime. Trials, testings, failures (including in marriage)—as well as triumphs—marked his days both before and after becoming the king of Israel. If you study David's life, you'll see that he believed and embraced the fact that God is sovereign. Even when his enemies caused him pain, David knew God still reigned supreme. Let's look next at a psalm in which David asked the Lord for healing.

Leader: Read Psalm 6:1–10 very slowly. As you do, have the group...

- *put a triangle over every reference to the Lord.*
- *underline every reference to David—every me, I, my.*
- *put a big check mark by any verse that you relate to or that you want the Lord to do for you.*

DISCUSS

- What was David's state in verses 1–7?

• What did David ask God to do?

• In what ways do you relate to David's status and requests of God?

• What shift do you notice in verse 8? Describe the change in David's perspective as recorded in verses 9–10. What does this tell you?

• If we compare this psalm to the practice of journaling, how does the day's journal begin and how does it end?

• Many psalms follow the same pattern. What might be some of the benefits of pouring out your heart to God on paper?

night I make my bed swim, I dissolve my couch with my tears.

7 My eye has wasted away with grief; it has become old because of all my adversaries.

8 Depart from me, all you who do iniquity, for the LORD has heard the voice of my weeping.

9 The LORD has heard my supplication, the LORD receives my prayer.

10 All my enemies will be ashamed and greatly dismayed; they shall turn back, they will suddenly be ashamed.

JOB 1:1–3, 13–22

¹ There was a man in the land of Uz whose name was Job; and that man was blameless, upright, fearing God and turning away from evil.

² Seven sons and three daughters were born to him.

³ His possessions also were 7,000 sheep, 3,000 camels, 500 yoke of oxen, 500 female donkeys, and very many servants; and that man was the greatest of all the men of the east....

¹³ Now on the day when his sons and his daughters were eating and drinking wine in their oldest brother's house,

OBSERVE

The book of Job details the account of a man who suffered excruciating pain emotionally, physically, and mentally—so much so that at one point Job wished he had never been born.

Maybe you feel that way yourself. Let's see what we can learn from Job that might give you hope for a better future in spite of your current anguish.

Leader: Read Job 1:1–3, 13–22 aloud.

• *Have the group underline every reference to* **Job**—*every* **man, him, his, he, you, your.**

DISCUSS

• Summarize what happened to Job in this single day.

14 a messenger came to Job and said, "The oxen were plowing and the donkeys feeding beside them,

15 and the Sabeans attacked and took them. They also slew the servants with the edge of the sword, and I alone have escaped to tell you."

16 While he was still speaking, another also came and said, "The fire of God fell from heaven and burned up the sheep and the servants and consumed them, and I alone have escaped to tell you."

17 While he was still speaking, another also came and said, "The Chaldeans formed three bands and made a raid on the camels

and took them and slew the servants with the edge of the sword, and I alone have escaped to tell you."

18 While he was still speaking, another also came and said, "Your sons and your daughters were eating and drinking wine in their oldest brother's house,

19 and behold, a great wind came from across the wilderness and struck the four corners of the house, and it fell on the young people and they died, and I alone have escaped to tell you."

20 Then Job arose and tore his robe and shaved his head, and he fell to the ground and worshiped.

• How did Job respond?

• What does this tell you about Job's faith, his relationship with God?

21 He said, "Naked I came from my mother's womb, and naked I shall return there. The LORD gave and the LORD has taken away. Blessed be the name of the LORD."

22 Through all this Job did not sin nor did he blame God.

OBSERVE

This was not the end of Job's troubles.

Leader: Read Job 2:1–3:1 aloud. Have the group do the following:
  • *Mark every reference to **Satan** with a pitchfork, like this:* ⑁
  • *Underline every reference to **Job**, including pronouns.*
  • *Circle the references to* Job's wife.
  • *Draw a wavy line under every reference to **Job's friends**, like this:* 〰

JOB 2:1—3:1

1 Again there was a day when the sons of God came to present themselves before the LORD, and Satan also came among them to present himself before the LORD.

2 The LORD said to Satan, "Where have you come from?" Then Satan answered the

LORD and said, "From roaming about on the earth and walking around on it."

3 The LORD said to Satan, "Have you considered My servant Job? For there is no one like him on the earth, a blameless and upright man fearing God and turning away from evil. And he still holds fast his integrity, although you incited Me against him to ruin him without cause."

4 Satan answered the LORD and said, "Skin for skin! Yes, all that a man has he will give for his life.

5 "However, put forth Your hand now, and touch his bone and his

DISCUSS

- What did you learn from marking the references to Satan?

- Is there any limitation on Satan's power? How do you know?

• What happened to Job's body?

• Was Job's wife any comfort? What did she suggest?

flesh; he will curse You to Your face."

6 So the LORD said to Satan, "Behold, he is in your power, only spare his life."

7 Then Satan went out from the presence of the LORD and smote Job with sore boils from the sole of his foot to the crown of his head.

8 And he took a potsherd to scrape himself while he was sitting among the ashes.

9 Then his wife said to him, "Do you still hold fast your integrity? Curse God and die!"

10 But he said to her, "You speak as one of the foolish women

speaks. Shall we indeed accept good from God and not accept adversity?" In all this Job did not sin with his lips.

11 Now when Job's three friends heard of all this adversity that had come upon him, they came each one from his own place, Eliphaz the Temanite, Bildad the Shuhite and Zophar the Naamathite; and they made an appointment together to come to sympathize with him and comfort him.

12 When they lifted up their eyes at a distance and did not recognize him, they raised their voices and wept. And each of

• How did Job's friends respond to Job when they saw him? What does this suggest about Job's condition?

• What did you learn from Job 3:1? How did Job feel about life?

• To what extent can you relate?

them tore his robe
and they threw dust
over their heads
toward the sky.

13 Then they sat
down on the ground
with him for seven
days and seven nights
with no one speaking a
word to him, for they
saw that his pain was
very great.

3:1 Afterward Job
opened his mouth and
cursed the day of his
birth.

OBSERVE

Have you ever been so miserable that you
wanted to die?

Leader: Read Job 6:8–10 aloud.
  • *Have the group underline every pronoun that refers to **Job,** who is speaking
  in this passage.*

JOB 6:8–10

8 Oh that my request
might come to pass,
and that God would
grant my longing!

9 Would that God
were willing to crush
me, that He would

loose His hand and cut me off!

10 But it is still my consolation, and I rejoice in unsparing pain, that I have not denied the words of the Holy One.

JOB 19:23–27

23 Oh that my words were written! Oh that they were inscribed in a book!

24 That with an iron stylus and lead they were engraved in the rock forever!

25 As for me, I know that my Redeemer lives, and at the last He will take His stand on the earth.

26 Even after my skin is destroyed, yet

DISCUSS

• What did you learn from marking the pronouns that refer to Job? What did he want God to do?

• What was Job's consolation?

• What does that tell you about Job?

OBSERVE

Job's pain was unsparing, yet he would not take his own life. Why?

Leader: Read Job 19:23–27 aloud. Have the group…
- *underline every reference to **Job**—every **me, I, my**.*
- *mark every reference to **Redeemer,** including the pronouns **He** and **His,** with a cross:* ✝

DISCUSS

• What did you learn from marking the references to Job?

• What did you learn from marking references to his Redeemer?

• Was there hope for Job? If so, from whom or what?

• Is there hope for you? If so, in whom or in what is your hope found?

OBSERVE

We always want to know how a story ends, don't we? The final outcome makes all the difference. Surely after divorce, you've wondered what will become of you, of your family? If you have hope, if you know there's a future, it's easier to persevere.

So what was the end of Job's story? Why did God put it in His book, the Bible? What is His lesson for you?

from my flesh I shall see God;

27 Whom I myself shall behold, and whom my eyes will see and not another.

JOB 42 (SELECTED VERSES)

1 Then Job answered the LORD and said,

2 "I know that You can do all things, and that no purpose of Yours can be thwarted.…

6 Therefore I retract, and I repent in dust and ashes."…

10 The LORD restored the fortunes of Job when he prayed for his friends, and the LORD increased all that Job had twofold.

11 Then all his brothers and all his sisters and all who had known him before came to him, and they ate bread with him in his house; and they consoled him and comforted him for all the adversities that the LORD had brought on him. And each one gave him one piece of money, and each a ring of gold.

12 The LORD blessed the latter days of Job more than his beginning....

Leader: Read aloud the selected verses from Job 42 and have the group...

- *underline every reference to **Job**, including pronouns.*
- *put a triangle over every reference to **the Lord**, including pronouns.*
- *draw a cloud around the word **purpose**, like this:*

DISCUSS

- What had Job learned about God, and what did it prompt him to do?

- What did the Lord do on Job's behalf, according to verse 10? When did God do this? In other words, what preceded His action?

- Have you prayed for your former spouse? (If not, read Job 42:7–10 sometime soon.)

- Look at all the places where you marked references to the Lord. What did God do for Job?

- How does the end of Job's story compare with the beginning? What or who brought about this outcome?

- What, if anything, have you observed in this true account that might give you hope after divorce?

16 After this, Job lived 140 years, and saw his sons and his grandsons, four generations.

17 And Job died, an old man and full of days.

OBSERVE

Are you thinking, *That was Job's end; what about me?* Let's read what the Bible says to you through the apostle Paul's words in Romans 8.

Leader: Read Romans 8:28–31 aloud. Have the group say aloud and…

- *underline every reference to* **those who love God,** *including all the* **those, these, we,** *and* **us.**
- *mark the phrase* **according to His purpose** *with a cloud.*

ROMANS 8:28–31

28 And we know that God causes all things to work together for good to those who love God, to those who are called according to His purpose.

29 For those whom He foreknew, He also predestined to become conformed to the image of His Son, so that He would be the firstborn among many brethren;

30 and these whom He predestined, He also called; and these whom He called, He also justified; and these whom He justified, He also glorified.

31 What then shall we say to these things? If God is for us, who is against us?

INSIGHT

The term *called,* in Romans 8:28, 30, is synonymous with being saved, being a follower of Christ. Those God calls He justifies—declares righteous—and glorifies. They will live with Him forever and ever in their immortal bodies.

DISCUSS

• What did you learn from marking the references to "those who love God"?

• What did you learn from marking *purpose,* both here in Romans and in the previous passage, Job 42:2?

• Did Paul say all things are good? What exactly is the promise of Romans 8:28?

• Would this promise cover even our wrong choices and the consequences they bring? What does the word *all* include?

- Who can claim the promise of Romans 8:28? Is it for everyone, or are there qualifications? If so, what are they?

- Sin brings a consequence, but how might God use the consequence to conform us "to the image of His Son"?

- What if you made a mistake and got a divorce when you knew you shouldn't? Does this promise still apply to you?

- How can your divorce be used to conform you to the image of Jesus?

- Does Romans 8:28 provide an excuse for sin? Why or why not?

- How does it change our perspective to think that God in His sovereignty might have a purpose in allowing something as bad as divorce?

- How might this give you hope?

WRAP IT UP

What kept Job alive in his pain was the knowledge of his Redeemer. Job's Redeemer lived, and Job knew he would someday see Him face to face in his brand-new resurrected body. Glorification was coming. That is why Job was able to exult in pain unsparing, why Job determined he would not deny the words of his God (Job 6:10).

Because Job persevered, he came to know God and himself even better. And God blessed the latter days of Job more than his beginning.

And what about you, beloved of God? How will you handle your pain? How will you get through your divorce? Will you believe God? Will you cling to His promise that this will work together for your good and His glory as you are conformed more and more into the image of His Son, the Lord Jesus Christ?

If you are God's child, His promise is yours. If you are not His, He wants you to be. This is why God sent His only begotten Son, born of a virgin, born without sin, into this world to pay for your sin in full by dying on a cross. Jesus came to redeem you from sin and death and offer you forgiveness of sins and the gift of eternal life. Think about it. Talk to God about it—and don't miss next week's study.

In the meantime, I invite you to visit our website where we've set up a special page for this study: http://precept.org/divorce. There you'll find an online community where you can participate by sharing with others the hope you're finding in God's Word and by praying for other individuals who are enduring the pain of divorce.

Divorce and the aftermath can be long and drawn out. Wearying. Draining. You want it to be gone from your life, from your mind. You just want to get it over with so you can get on with life—if there is life after divorce.

The question then becomes, how can you find the power to go on, to endure this painful, exhausting experience?

Let's see what God's Word says.

OBSERVE

When the apostle Paul wrote 2 Corinthians in the Bible, he bared his soul in a way we don't see in any of his other letters. What a blessing to those of us who have despaired of our lives, our futures, for any reason.

As Paul brought his letter to a close, it's as if the Spirit of God directed him to let all be known. To hold nothing back in respect to the trials he had endured and how the Lord had taken him through them.

Paul had an incredible experience of being caught up into heaven. Consequently, in order to keep the apostle from boasting about the experience, God permitted a messenger from Satan to give him a thorn in his flesh. (Can you relate?) Three times Paul asked God to take it away, and each time God's answer was no. (Have you, too, prayed for relief but God hasn't resolved the situation the way you wanted Him to?)

So what did Paul do in the light of God's answer? Let's see what we can learn that will help you.

2 CORINTHIANS 12:9–10

⁹ And He has said to me, "My grace is sufficient for you, for power is perfected in weakness." Most gladly, therefore, I will rather boast about my weaknesses, so that the power of Christ may dwell in me.

¹⁰ Therefore I am well content with weaknesses, with insults, with distresses, with persecutions, with difficulties, for Christ's sake; for when I am weak, then I am strong.

Leader: Read 2 Corinthians 12:9–10 slowly. *Have the group do the following:*

- *Underline every pronoun referring to **Paul**, who in this passage was describing his conversation with God.*
- *Mark each occurrence of **therefore** with three dots in the shape of a triangle, like this:*
- *Mark the words **weakness** and **weak** with a semicircle:*

INSIGHT

In 2 Corinthians 12:9, the Greek verb form translated as "has said" is in the perfect tense, which indicates a past completed action with a present or continuous result. So in essence the Lord was saying to Paul, "This is My final answer. Don't ask again." But the exciting part is what came along with the no. Read carefully the second part of God's answer.

DISCUSS

• What was God's final answer to Paul? Discuss all of what He said. What would help Paul live with this thorn?

• What was Paul's response to God? Or to put it another way, why the *therefores* in these two verses? *Therefore* is a term of conclusion; what was Paul's conclusion in verse 9?

• What was Paul's conclusion in verse 10?

• Look at the list of things Paul said he would be content in. Which of these can you relate to?

• What did you learn from marking *weaknesses, weak*?

OBSERVE

Leader: Read 2 Corinthians 12:9–10 again.

  • *This time have the group draw a stick of dynamite over each occurrence of the words **power** and **strong**, like this:*

DISCUSS

• What did you learn from marking these words?

• Why is there strength in weakness for the child of God?

• What must you do in your situation if you believe this?

OBSERVE

Let's look at another passage in 2 Corinthians that will give us a better understanding of what Paul actually experienced. What you are about to read was in response to some people in the church at Corinth who were giving Paul a hard time, saying he wasn't even a true apostle and shouldn't be ministering. They criticized his appearance, his speech, his supposed failure to fulfill his promise, and more.

Maybe since your divorce you've experienced similar rejection, condemnation, judgment—bad press—from people who claim to love Christ. If so, you'll relate.

Leader: Read 2 Corinthians 11:22–29. Have the group...

- *underline any of **Paul's experiences that you've felt or experienced in some form.***
- *mark **weak** and **weakness** with a semicircle, as before.*

2 CORINTHIANS 11:22–29

22 Are they Hebrews? So am I. Are they Israelites? So am I. Are they descendants of Abraham? So am I.

23 Are they servants of Christ?—I speak as if insane—I more so; in far more labors, in far more imprisonments, beaten times without number, often in danger of death.

24 Five times I received from the Jews thirty-nine lashes.

25 Three times I was beaten with rods, once I was stoned, three times I was shipwrecked, a night and a day I have spent in the deep.

26 I have been on frequent journeys, in

dangers from rivers, dangers from robbers, dangers from my countrymen, dangers from the Gentiles, dangers in the city, dangers in the wilderness, dangers on the sea, dangers among false brethren;

27 I have been in labor and hardship, through many sleepless nights, in hunger and thirst, often without food, in cold and exposure.

28 Apart from such external things, there is the daily pressure on me of concern for all the churches.

29 Who is weak without my being weak? Who is led into sin without my intense concern?

DISCUSS

• Without discussing each thing Paul endured, what does this passage tell you about Paul's life, and how can it help you with the painful situations you've faced or are facing in your divorce?

• Children are greatly impacted by divorce (whether friendly or unfriendly), sometimes witnessing quarrels, possibly experiencing abuse, often worrying about their future or their supposed role in the divorce. Reread verses 28–29 in the light of your concern for your children and the trauma of divorce. What sort of "daily pressure" of concern do you feel?

• So from just what you've seen this far in this lesson, where can you find hope? Where can you find relief from the pain and pressure of your circumstances?

OBSERVE

Do you wonder how Paul endured all these things without breaking or becoming bitter? Let's find out.

Leader: Read 2 Corinthians 4:17–18 slowly. Have the group…
* *underline the pronouns **we** and **us.***
* *mark the word **affliction,** with a jagged line, like this:* /\/\/\/

DISCUSS

* How did Paul view his affliction? What words did he use to describe it?

* How does that strike you in light of the list of his sufferings you just read in 2 Corinthians 11:22–29?

* Obviously few of us have experienced the hardships Paul endured, but in his life we can find lessons for our own suffering. What did you read in 2 Corinthians 4:17–18 that shows how Paul handled his experiences?

2 CORINTHIANS 4:17–18

17 For momentary, light affliction is producing for us an eternal weight of glory far beyond all comparison,

18 while we look not at the things which are seen, but at the things which are not seen; for the things which are seen are temporal, but the things which are not seen are eternal.

• What application, if any, do you find here for your situation?

ROMANS 8:9b, 14

⁹ But if anyone does not have the Spirit of Christ, he does not belong to Him....

¹⁴ For all who are being led by the Spirit of God, these are sons of God.

ACTS 1:8

But you will receive power when the Holy Spirit has come upon you; and you shall be My witnesses both in Jerusalem, and in all Judea and Samaria, and even to the remotest part of the earth.

OBSERVE

Where did Paul's power come from, and what continued recharging the batteries of his power? What was the source of his ability to endure afflictions with hope? This is what we want to explore next.

Leader: Read Romans 8:9b, 14 and Acts 1:8. Have the group...

• *draw a cloud around every reference to **the Spirit**.*

• *mark **power** with a stick of dynamite:*

DISCUSS

• What did you learn from marking *the Spirit*?

• How would you describe your relationship to the Spirit of God?

• The Spirit of God through His power
makes us witnesses of Jesus. What might
that look like in the process of divorce?

OBSERVE

How does a person get the Spirit of God?

*Leader: Read Ephesians 1:13–14. Have the
group...*

- *underline every* **you, your, our.**
- *mark every reference to* **the Spirit of
God,** *including* **who,** *with a cloud.*

DISCUSS

• What did you learn from marking *you*
and *your*?

• Did you notice the word *after* and the
tenses of the verbs, which indicate a pro-
gression of events leading to our being
sealed with the Spirit? Discuss and then
number the events as they seem to occur.

EPHESIANS 1:13–14

¹³ In Him [Jesus],
you also, after listening
to the message of
truth, the gospel of
your salvation—having
also believed, you were
sealed in Him with the
Holy Spirit of
promise,

¹⁴ who is given as a
pledge of our inheri-
tance, with a view to
the redemption of
God's own possession,
to the praise of His
glory.

INSIGHT

The word *pledge* in Ephesians 1:14 could also be translated as "guarantee."

When you think of being sealed in Christ by the Spirit of God, just imagine the seal under the lid of instant coffee. The unbroken seal guarantees that no one has contaminated the coffee, no one has tampered with it since it left the factory.

When Paul mentioned "the redemption of God's own possession, to the praise of His glory," he was referring to the eventual resurrection of our bodies when mortal puts on immortality, and corruptible becomes incorruptible. (All of this is taught in greater detail in 1 Corinthians 15, the resurrection chapter.)

• So what did you learn from marking the references to the Holy Spirit? What is the connection between our belief and His presence?

OBSERVE

So often, divorces are extremely traumatic. In our pain, we're tempted to treat each other like dirt, to walk all over each other because of what has happened, what has been said. But can we find a way to glorify God in midst of our suffering, to harness our hurt and anger and live life on a higher plane? To walk in the power of His Spirit?

Leader: Read Galatians 5:16–17 and 22–26 aloud. Have the group...

- *put a cloud around every reference to* **the Spirit.**
- *underline every reference to* **those who belong to Christ,** *including the pronouns* **you, we,** *and* **us.**

Leader: Now read the text again.

- *This time have the group read it aloud with you and put a big* **X** *over every reference to* **the flesh.**

GALATIANS 5:16–17, 22–26

16 But I say, walk by the Spirit, and you will not carry out the desire of the flesh.

17 For the flesh sets its desire against the Spirit, and the Spirit against the flesh; for these are in opposition to one another, so that you may not do the things that you please....

22 But the fruit of the Spirit is love, joy, peace, patience, kindness, goodness, faithfulness,

23 gentleness, self-control; against such things there is no law.

24 Now those who belong to Christ Jesus

have crucified the flesh with its passions and desires.

25 If we live by the Spirit, let us also walk by the Spirit.

26 Let us not become boastful, challenging one another, envying one another.

INSIGHT

In Galatians 5:16, the Greek verb used in the phrase *walk by the Spirit* is in the present tense. This implies habitual or continual action. Therefore, it could read this way, "keep on walking in the Spirit and you will not carry out the desire of the flesh." How encouraging! Though the flesh desires to have its way, God assures us that we can conquer the desires of the flesh by continuing to let the Spirit put us in overdrive, so to speak.

DISCUSS

• What did you learn about the flesh and the Spirit and their relationship to one another?

• So what is your duty as a child of God when the desires of your flesh conflict with the Spirit?

• According to verses 22–23, what does it look like, how do we behave when the Spirit, rather than the flesh, is in control of us?

• What did you learn from verse 25? Practically speaking, what does it mean to "walk by the Spirit"?

• How would all this help in dealing with your former spouse?

WRAP IT UP

Life is not easy, is it, beloved? It is not a simple thing to love others as God instructs, especially when someone hurts us deeply. But you can do it, because God Himself lives inside you and you have His Spirit.

We need to remember that the closer we come to the return of Jesus Christ, the rougher life is going to get—especially for those who love and truly follow Him. As Paul wrote to Timothy in his final letter, "But realize this, that in the last days difficult times will come" (2 Timothy 3:1).

Yet it is in the trials, the tests, and the difficulties of life that God proves Himself to be all that He says He is and all He promises to be as our heavenly Father. Many who have been through horrendous situations say, "I wouldn't trade what I learned, what I experienced with God in this trial. It was worth the pain, the hurt because I have come to know Him in a way I otherwise never would have known."

Beloved of God, you will find your current pain is worth all you will gain from Him. If you'll walk in His power, by His Spirit, God will use it all to conform you into the glorious image of His Son, our Lord and Savior Jesus Christ.

You might want to memorize what Paul wrote to the Corinthians: "But by the grace of God I am what I am, and His grace toward me did not prove vain; but I labored even more than all of them, yet not I, but the grace of God with me" (1 Corinthians 15:10).

Feelings can be incredibly powerful, can't they? What do you do with all your emotions? Do you have your act together? In the midst of this uprooting because of your divorce, are you functioning as God intends?

Or are you hurt, angry, bitter, frustrated, plotting how to get even? Or perhaps you're feeling utterly defeated, unloved, and maybe even unlovable?

All of these are the natural, normal reactions of our flesh to disappointment and hurt. It's understandable that you feel fragile emotionally and physically. However, you don't want these dark emotions to consume you or to drive you to do or say things you'll regret, especially if your former spouse has become an adversary.

So let's get hold of some solid biblical truth that can strengthen and carry you through this trauma. Let's learn how you can take control rather than letting your emotions hold sway, as we consider how God wants you to treat your ex, even if he or she has become your enemy.

The principles we'll look at this week assume that you are a genuine follower of Jesus Christ; however, if that is not the case and even if you don't know much about Christianity, it's okay. Hang in there with me. Be assured God has answers for you and that is why you are holding this book in your hands. Just remember, even if you don't like or agree with the verses we'll be reading together, they are God's words, taken straight from the Bible. God cannot lie. His are words of life that will get you through this situation if you'll listen, believe, and do what He says.

So give God a chance. You have absolutely nothing to lose and a future to gain.

EPHESIANS 4:1–2

¹ Therefore I, the prisoner of the Lord, implore you to walk in a manner worthy of the calling with which you have been called,

② ² with all humility and gentleness, with patience, showing tolerance for one another in love.

OBSERVE

The new converts in the cosmopolitan city of Ephesus were in the midst of an adverse situation. Among other things, marriages and morals were challenged continuously. It was critical that these new Christians learned to live above the circumstances, contrary to the godless culture, in order to demonstrate the power Jesus gives to His children when they walk under the control of His Spirit.

What does that look like? Let's see for ourselves.

Leader: *Read Ephesians 4:1–2.*
   • *Have the group underline every occurrence of **you.***

INSIGHT

The calling mentioned here is a reference to the fact that God has called you to be His child through faith in Jesus Christ. According to Ephesians 1:3–4, God chose you for Himself before the foundation of the world.

DISCUSS

• What did you learn from underlining *you*?

• What do you think it means to walk "worthy of the calling"?

• What does that walk look like? Number the things listed in verse 2. (The first, humility, is already numbered for you.) Then discuss each behavior briefly and how this might affect your interactions with your former spouse, your children, relatives, and others affected by your divorce.

• What are some of the emotions you find yourself dealing with as a result of your divorce? How would obeying these verses from Ephesians help you handle those emotions?

• When you think of showing tolerance in love toward your ex, does it seem impossible? How can you do that when you don't feel love? Read the Insight box on the following page and then discuss how this instruction applies in divorce.

INSIGHT

Agape, the Greek word translated in Ephesians 4:2 as "love," describes God's kind of love. It is unmerited in that it is not based on another's qualities or actions. Agape is the love that loved us when we were sinners, helpless, ungodly, God's enemies (Romans 5:6–11). Agape love is objective. It knows all about you and yet desires your highest good and loves before the love is returned (1 John 4:7–21).

EPHESIANS 4:22–27

22 that, in reference to your former manner of life, you lay aside the old self, which is being corrupted in accordance with the lusts of deceit,

OBSERVE

In this next passage we will look at what God tells us about our natural fleshly instincts—instincts that can really lead us into trouble if we let them have their way!

Leader: Read Ephesians 4:22–27 aloud. Have the group say aloud and mark the key words and phrases as indicated:

- *Underline every occurrence of the pronouns **your, you,** and **we**.*
- *Put a big **X** over **the old self**.*
- *Put a check mark over **the new self**.*

INSIGHT

The *old self* in this passage is a reference to what you were before you became a Christian, before you were saved. This is the old you that died so that you would be raised up with Christ and become a new creation in Him. As a new creation, you now have power over sin and over the flesh through God's Spirit, as you saw last week. The *new self* is you with the Spirit living inside and giving you His power.

Remember, God's Holy Spirit is the One who gives you love, joy, peace, patience, kindness, goodness, faithfulness, gentleness, and self-control whenever you let Him (Galatians 5:22–23)! As a Christian, it's always a matter of choice as to who will control you: the Spirit or the flesh.

23 and that you be renewed in the spirit of your mind,

24 and put on the new self, which in the likeness of God has been created in righteousness and holiness of the truth.

25 Therefore, laying aside falsehood, speak truth each one of you with his neighbor, for we are members of one another.

26 Be angry, and yet do not sin; do not let the sun go down on your anger,

27 and do not give the devil an opportunity.

DISCUSS

• What did you learn from marking the pronouns referring to the believer? Take it verse by verse, and discuss what each reference reveals.

• What did you learn about the *old self* and the *new self*?

• What are God's instructions in verses 25–27?

• Did you see the *therefore* in verse 25? As we noted earlier, *therefore* is a term of conclusion, so we should always pause to see what the *therefore* is there for! What do you learn? Is it possible to obey the instructions in verses 25–27? Explain your answer.

• So is anger wrong? Shouldn't we be angry at sin, at injustice, at corruption, at betrayal? If so, how are we to deal with that anger? How will knowing this help you in dealing with your ex?

INSIGHT

If you do a word study on *anger* throughout the Old and New Testaments, you'll discover that God is the One who is angered the most! Sin, unrighteousness, injustice, meanness, hypocrisy, and other evils anger God. His is a righteous anger—indignation at the wrongful and unjust behavior of mankind.

- Talk in practical terms about how the devil could gain an opportunity to do what the devil does! What are some ways we give him a foothold in our lives?

- How can holding on to anger affect your mind? What can the devil do with unresolved anger?

- Did you notice what Ephesians 4:23 says about your mind? The mind can be the devil's playground. What are some of the battles fought in your mind since your divorce? (Many times when we have the courage to share, it gives others courage!)

EPHESIANS 4:29–5:2

29 Let no unwholesome word proceed from your mouth, but only such a word as is good for edification according to the need of the moment, so that it will give grace to those who hear.

30 Do not grieve the Holy Spirit of God, by whom you were sealed for the day of redemption.

31 Let all bitterness and wrath and anger and clamor and slander be put away from you, along with all malice.

32 Be kind to one another, tenderhearted, forgiving each other, just as God in

OBSERVE

God has more to tell us in Ephesians about how to live so that we won't later regret our choices.

Leader: Read Ephesians 4:29–5:2 aloud. Have the group...

- *underline **every instruction** in these verses (just the instruction itself, not any explanation that accompanies it).*
- *put a box around the phrases **so that** and **just as**.*
- *put a big **X** over the words **forgiving** and **forgiven**.*

INSIGHT

When we believe on Jesus Christ, we are given the gift of the Holy Spirit of God. God's indwelling Spirit is our ticket, so to speak, who gets us into heaven. He is the guarantee that one day—the day of redemption—we will each have a new body and live forever with Jesus.

DISCUSS

• Discuss one by one the instructions in this passage and how each particular command would or would not apply to you as a divorced person.

• In Ephesians 4:25 God tells us to speak the truth. Now, in verse 29 He gives further instructions on our speech. What did you learn about the importance of your words *to* the one who divorced you? Your words *about* him or her?

• What did you learn from verses 31–32 about how God wants you to respond to your ex?

• If you are a Christian, does your behavior have any effect on God's Spirit, who lives in you? Explain your answer.

• Read verse 32 aloud. What do you learn about forgiveness? What truth did marking *just as* bring to light?

Christ also has forgiven you.

5:1 Therefore be imitators of God, as beloved children;

2 and walk in love, just as Christ also loved you and gave Himself up for us, an offering and a sacrifice to God as a fragrant aroma.

• Should you forgive the one who divorced you? Why or why not?

• Do you think it is possible to walk in love toward the one who divorced you? Why or why not?

• How do you think you would feel if you obeyed these instructions? Would you feel like a victim or like a conqueror? Would obedience make you feel as if you're being controlled by the behavior of another person? Or would obedience put you in control of the situation? Discuss this.

OBSERVE

What are you going to do if your former spouse behaves like an enemy or treats you as an enemy? Let's look at some practical precepts from God's Word that will help you treat your ex-husband, your ex-wife in a way that honors God, even if that individual is not treating you as he or she should.

Although extenuating circumstances— such as some sort of danger to you or the children, possible abuse, violence, untoward threats, unfair financial dealings—might change the parameters, let's look to God's Word for general guiding principles.

OBSERVE

Leader: *Read Romans 12:17–21. Have the group…*

- *put a box around every reference to **evil***.

- *underline **every instruction**—but only the instruction, not any explanation that goes with it.*

DISCUSS

- What instructions did you find in these verses?

- Whose instructions are these? Where did they come from?

- What did you learn about God, the Lord, in verse 19?

ROMANS 12:17–21

17 Never pay back evil for evil to anyone. Respect what is right in the sight of all men.

18 If possible, so far as it depends on you, be at peace with all men.

19 Never take your own revenge, beloved, but leave room for the wrath of God, for it is written, "Vengeance is mine, I will repay," says the Lord.

20 "But if your enemy is hungry, feed him, and if he is

thirsty, give him a drink; for in so doing you will heap burning coals on his head."

21 Do not be overcome by evil, but overcome evil with good.

• As a divorced person, what is your responsibility to your ex-wife or ex-husband?

• What is God's responsibility?

• Are these instructions easy to follow? Is it possible for you to do this? Explain your answer.

MATTHEW 5:43–48

43 You have heard that it was said, "You shall love your neighbor and hate your enemy."

44 But I say to you, love your enemies and pray for those who persecute you,

OBSERVE

During Jesus' earthly ministry He constantly had to deal with people who were enemies, men bent on His destruction. As the One who appears in the presence of God to intercede for you, Jesus knows what you are experiencing and He has some instructions for how you, as His follower, should conduct yourself. Let's wrap up this week's lesson by looking at the instructions He's given us.

Leader: Read Matthew 5:43–48 and Luke 6:31, 35–37 aloud. Have the group...

- *underline every occurrence of __you__ and __your__.*
- *mark each reference to __love__ with a heart:* ♡
- *put a triangle over every reference to __God__, including pronouns and the synonyms __your Father__ and __Most High__.*

DISCUSS

- Discuss, verse by verse, what you learned from marking each occurrence of *you* and *your.*

- Who is to be your role model, your example to follow? What example has this role model set?

- Do you think these instructions would pertain to you in the treatment of your ex? If not, why? If so, how?

45 so that you may be sons of your Father who is in heaven; for He causes His sun to rise on the evil and the good, and sends rain on the righteous and the unrighteous.

46 For if you love those who love you, what reward do you have? Do not even the tax collectors do the same?

47 If you greet only your brothers, what more are you doing than others? Do not even the Gentiles do the same?

48 Therefore you are to be perfect, as your heavenly Father is perfect.

LUKE 6:31, 35–37

31 Treat others the same way you want them to treat you....

35 But love your enemies, and do good, and lend, expecting nothing in return; and your reward will be great, and you will be sons of the Most High; for He Himself is kind to ungrateful and evil men.

36 Be merciful, just as your Father is merciful.

37 Do not judge, and you will not be judged; and do not condemn, and you will not be condemned; pardon, and you will be pardoned.

• Did you notice the instruction to pray for those who persecute you (Matthew 5:44)? Whether or not your ex is persecuting you, do you think God wants you to pray for him or her? Explain your answer.

Leader: Invite the group members to discuss how they feel about this and to share anything they have learned by praying for their ex-wife or ex-husband.

• What concerns or fears do you have about what might happen if you treat your ex-husband or ex-wife as Jesus instructs?

Leader: Encourage the group members to share their concerns aloud so that you can help one another reason this out together. Just remember, there is not always a pat answer, as the whole situation needs to be considered. Scripture is not to be read in isolation but to be considered along with the whole counsel of God.

WRAP IT UP

One of the exciting benefits of belonging to God is that you know truth—and truth sets us free. You also have God's Spirit, who not only leads you into all truth, but also enables you by His power and His indwelling presence to live according to His Word.

If you have Jesus, then you can choose to live a life of self-control. Because Jesus Christ is in you and you are in Him, you don't need to live as you used to live—apart from Jesus Christ—nor treat your enemies as they treat you. No matter your situation, beloved, you can walk in a way that pleases God.

Consequently, there is hope even after divorce—hope for living in victory as more than a conqueror. Never forget who you are as a child of God. You are beloved of God, imbued with the knowledge and power of God that enables you to live as an overcomer (1 John 5:1–4). Remember that you are never a victim!

So listen and hear with your heart the prayer God led Paul to pray for His beloved children:

> For this reason I bow my knees before the Father, from whom every family in heaven and on earth derives its name, that He would grant you, according to the riches of His glory, to be strengthened with power through His Spirit in the inner man, so that Christ may dwell in your hearts through faith; and that you, being rooted and grounded in love, may be able to comprehend with all the saints what is the breadth and length and height and

depth, and to know the love of Christ which surpasses knowledge, that you may be filled up to all the fullness of God.

Now to Him who is able to do far more abundantly beyond all that we ask or think, according to the power that works within us, to Him be the glory in the church and in Christ Jesus to all generations forever and ever. Amen. (Ephesians 3:14–21)

With divorce can come all sorts of threats, fears, insecurities, and a terrible feeling of aloneness.

You cannot help but wonder what's going to happen to you. Who will take care of you? How can you survive on your own? How can you make it financially?

It can feel overwhelming. Absolutely, totally overwhelming.

So how will you deal with it? Where can you turn to find calm in this storm? All sorts of suggestions may come your way.

"Take a little drink. It will calm you."

"This is huge. Don't be afraid to take a pill or two to help you. Get a prescription until you get over the trauma of it all."

Or you may come up with your own ideas for numbing the pain.

You might decide to eat whatever you want and as much as you want. Or you might stay in bed as long as you can, sleeping away the hours because your dreams are better than your life. (This is what I did! I wasn't a Christian when I got divorced.)

You might retreat into novels or movies, pour yourself into your children, seek solace from a friend, bury yourself in your career, or seek the company of that person who seemed interested in pursuing a relationship.

But what if instead you turn to the Wonderful Counselor who was given to you when you became a child of God (Isaiah 9:6)? The one who is waiting for you to give it all to Him?

What if you make Him your all in all, your place of security and refuge?

JEREMIAH 17:5–6

5 Thus says the LORD, "Cursed is the man who trusts in mankind and makes flesh his strength, and whose heart turns away from the LORD.

6 "For he will be like a bush in the desert and will not see when prosperity comes, but will live in stony wastes in the wilderness, a land of salt without inhabitant."

OBSERVE

When a test comes our way, unless we have matured greatly in our relationship with God, our *first* tendency is to turn to another warm body for help, comfort, or wisdom. Certainly friends play an important role in a healthy life. But is that where God wants us to go *first*?

Leader: Read Jeremiah 17:5–6 aloud slowly.

• *Have the group put a big* **X** *over the references to* **the man** *described in these verses. Include all pronouns such as* **his, he, whose.**

DISCUSS

• What did you learn about this man? How is he described?

• Where is his trust? Where will that lead? What kind of a life will he experience?

OBSERVE

Leader: Read Jeremiah 17:7–8. This time have the group say aloud and...

- *underline every reference to **the man,** including pronouns.*

- *mark every reference to **the tree,** including pronouns, like this:*

DISCUSS

- Now what did you learn about this man?

- What kind of a tree is he like? Discuss what you learned about the tree.

- Why does this tree survive in drought?

- Why is the stream important? What does a stream provide?

- So what would the stream in verse 8 parallel, and what is the lesson for our lives?

- What happens to this person when the heat is turned up, and why?

JEREMIAH 17:7–8

7 "Blessed is the man who trusts in the LORD and whose trust is the LORD.

8 "For he will be like a tree planted by the water, that extends its roots by a stream and will not fear when the heat comes; but its leaves will be green, and it will not be anxious in a year of drought nor cease to yield fruit."

Psalm 139:23–24

23 Search me,
O God, and know
my heart; try me and
know my anxious
thoughts;

24 and see if there be
any hurtful way in me,
and lead me in the
everlasting way.

Psalm 62:8

Trust in Him at all
times, O people; pour
out your heart before
Him; God is a refuge
for us.

OBSERVE

Leader: *Read Psalm 139:23–24 and Psalm 62:8. Have the group…*
- *underline every reference to the **humans** in these verses—**me, my, people, your, us.***
- *mark every reference to **God,** including the pronoun **Him,** with a triangle.*
- *put a heart over every occurrence of the word **heart.***

DISCUSS

- What did you learn from underlining every reference to the people in these verses?

- What did the psalmist ask God to do in Psalm 139:23–24, and why?

- What role does the heart play in these verses? What is the significance of this?

- What did you learn about God?

- Is God able to do, to be, the things the psalmist asked of Him?

- When you get anxious about your divorce, or your mind plays reruns of the footage of your relationship or a recent conversation with your ex, what do you need to do?

- Have you ever simply quieted yourself when you are anxious, told the Lord how you feel, then sat before the Lord and waited in silence? What happened? What came to mind?

- Sitting quietly, waiting, listening to God is a lost art in our busy lives but so beneficial. As you wait expectantly, God eventually will bring what He wants to your mind. You will recognize it is from Him because it will never be contrary to His Word, His character, His ways. Waiting on Him will, as Isaiah 40:31 says, renew your strength and fit you for the tasks ahead.

HEBREWS 13:5–6

5 Make sure that your character is free from the love of money, being content with what you have; for He Himself has said, "I will never desert you, nor will I ever forsake you,"

6 so that we confidently say, "The LORD is my helper, I will not be afraid. What will man do to me?"

HEBREWS 11:6

Without faith it is impossible to please Him, for he who comes to God must believe that He is and that He is a rewarder of those who seek Him.

OBSERVE

Divorce can bring all sorts of fears in respect to your future. You wonder, *Who is going to take care of me now, be there for me, protect me?* Divorced or married, the answer is fundamentally the same: God !

Leader: Read Hebrews 13:5–6 and 11:6 aloud with the group. Then read it again and have the group...

- *underline every reference to us as* **believers—your, you, we, my, I, me, those.**
- *put a triangle over every reference to* **God, the Lord,** *including pronouns.*

DISCUSS

- What did you learn from marking the references to God?

- What did you learn from marking the references to believers?

- Now what is your responsibility and what is God's? How would this look practically in any given situation?

OBSERVE

Leader: Read Luke 12:4–7, 22–24, 32 aloud and have the group…

- *Underline every reference to **the ones Jesus is addressing** in this passage.*

- *Put a jagged circle around every reference to **fear** or **being afraid,** like this:*

DISCUSS

- What was Jesus saying to His friends? (If you are a believer, a child of God, you are a friend [John 15:13–16].)

LUKE 12:4–7, 22–24, 32

4 "I say to you, My friends, do not be afraid of those who kill the body and after that have no more that they can do.

5 "But I will warn you whom to fear: fear the One who, after He has killed, has authority to cast into hell; yes, I tell you, fear Him!

6 "Are not five sparrows sold for two cents? Yet not one of them is forgotten before God.

7 "Indeed, the very hairs of your head are all numbered. Do not fear; you are more valuable than many sparrows."…

22 And He said to His disciples, "For this reason I say to you, do not worry about your life, as to what you will eat; nor for your body, as to what you will put on.

23 "For life is more than food, and the body more than clothing.

24 "Consider the ravens, for they neither sow nor reap; they have no storeroom nor barn, and yet God feeds them; how much more valuable you are than the birds!...

32 "Do not be afraid, little flock, for your Father has chosen gladly to give you the kingdom."

• What did you learn from marking *afraid* and *fear*?

• What comparisons did Jesus use to give assurance to God's friends, His flock?

OBSERVE

The book of Philippians is a letter written by the apostle Paul during his imprisonment in Rome. It is often referred to as the epistle, or letter, of joy. What counsel did this prisoner in chains give to the Christians in Philippi, and how can it point you toward help and hope after divorce?

Leader: Read Philippians 4:4–7 aloud together so the group can become familiar with its content. Then read it again slowly and have the group...

- *underline each **direct instruction.***
- *mark every reference to **the Lord, God** with a triangle.*
- *put a cross over the reference to **Christ Jesus.***

DISCUSS

- What are some of the anxieties you've had to deal with, especially in connection with your divorce?

PHILIPPIANS 4:4–7

4 Rejoice in the Lord always; again I will say, rejoice!

5 Let your gentle spirit be known to all men. The Lord is near.

6 Be anxious for nothing, but in everything by prayer and supplication with thanksgiving let your requests be made known to God.

7 And the peace of God, which surpasses all comprehension, will guard your hearts and your minds in Christ Jesus.

• What were Paul's instructions to the church at Philippi? Look at them in the order they are given, because there is a purpose in the order.

• What is the first instruction in verse 4? Discuss exactly what you are being instructed to do and for how long.

• Would doing this make people wonder about you? Where would obeying put your focus?

• Think of what you've learned about God
these past few weeks. What truths, if any,
have you read about God that would help
you to rejoice? Discuss your answer.

• Now, look carefully at verse 5. Why are
you to have a gentle spirit? How can you
do that?

INSIGHT

The Greek word for "gentle" is hard
to translate into English. It's been
translated as "forbearance, reason-
ableness." The word has to do with
yielding one's personal rights out of
consideration for others.

Leader: *Have the group read verse 6 aloud,*
then slowly read the Insight box on the follow-
ing page so they grasp exactly what they are to
do when they are anxious about anything.

INSIGHT

The Greek word translated as "prayer" in Philippians 4:6 indicates general prayer versus specific requests. In other words, it would be talking to God about who He is, what He has promised, what He did for others as recorded in the Bible. This kind of prayer involves praising God by declaring truths that address your needs for a particular situation. This puts your focus on the One who is omnipotent, who says that He is the Lord and nothing is too difficult for Him (Jeremiah 32:27). It's like general worship, acknowledging who God is and that He rules!

By contrast, the word translated as "supplication" in Philippians 4:6 focuses on specific requests that you want to lay before God. It describes petition, bringing your children, your finances, your fears, your insecurities before God. Nothing is too great or too small—not even asking for parking places! We are to live in total dependence on our heavenly Father, just as Jesus did.

• So what comes after taking a deep breath and getting that calm spirit? You stop being anxious—that is what the verb form implies. In other words, you are to remain calm no matter what. And how do you do that? What is the next instruction in verse 6? And how is this to be carried out?

• Why is all this to be done with thanksgiving? What does thanksgiving show?

• And according to verse 7, what will be the result of your obedience?

INSIGHT

Guard is a military term that means "to throw up a wall of protection that cannot be penetrated." Don't get off your knees until you have that unshakable peace, that unyielding confidence. Then do whatever God by His Spirit leads you to do.

• What did you learn about the Lord from these verses?

PHILIPPIANS 4:8–9

8 Finally, brethren, whatever is true,① whatever is honorable, whatever is right, whatever is pure, whatever is lovely, whatever is of good repute, if there is any excellence and if anything worthy of praise, dwell on these things.

9 The things you have learned and received and heard and seen in me, practice these things, and the God of peace will be with you.

OBSERVE

For humans the greatest battleground is *the mind*, often called *the heart* in Scripture. In the book of Proverbs we read that as a person thinks in their heart, so they are (23:7). Therefore we need to guard our thoughts very carefully so they won't run amuck and cause us all sorts of grave problems. This can be especially true in divorce. How do we do this? Let's see what Paul says.

Leader: *Read Philippians 4:8–9 aloud with the group. Then read it again and have the group…*
   • *underline each reference to the* **brethren,** *including the pronoun* **you.**
   • *put a triangle over* **God.**

Leader: *Read it again.*
   • *This time have the group put a number above each of the things we are to dwell on, to think about. The first one has been numbered for them.*

DISCUSS

- What are we instructed to center our minds on in these verses?

- What is the promise to those who do?

- So when a thought comes to your mind, take it through a security check. Pat it down. According to what God says, what thoughts will pass the security check? If a thought doesn't qualify, what should you do?

- Did Paul know what he was talking about? Explain your answer.

- How can these two verses help you heal from divorce?

PHILIPPIANS 4:10-14, 19

10 But I rejoiced in the Lord greatly, that now at last you have revived your concern for me; indeed, you were concerned before, but you lacked opportunity.

11 Not that I speak from want, for I have learned to be content in whatever circum-stances I am.

12 I know how to get along with humble means, and I also know how to live in prosperity; in any and every circumstance I have learned the secret of being filled and going hungry, both of having abundance and suffering need.

OBSERVE

Divorce can bring all sorts of fears. *Who's going to take care of me now that I'm divorced? How will I make it financially?** Let's see what additional help we can find in Paul's letter to the Philippians.

Leader: Read Philippians 4:10–14, 19 slowly. Have the group…
* *underline every pronoun referring to* **Paul**—*every* **I, me, my.**
* *circle each pronoun referring to* **the Philippians**—**you** *and* **your.**

DISCUSS

* What did you learn from marking the references to Paul?

* According to verse 12, how bad did things get for him?

---

* If you are struggling with fears, you'll find wisdom and help in the 40-minute Bible study *Breaking Free from Fear.*

• What did Paul learn? What does this suggest about how you can experience contentment? Does it come naturally, automatically? Explain your answer.

• How can you "get along with humble means" if financial challenges result from your divorce?

• What was Paul's secret for every circumstance?

• What did you learn from marking the references to the Philippians?

• What, if anything, did you learn in these verses about how God uses the body of Christ to accomplish His will, to fulfill His promises?

• Describe a time when God used you in this way.

• How can what you've seen in Philippians 4 help you with the challenges you face in your divorce?

13 I can do all things through Him who strengthens me.

14 Nevertheless, you have done well to share with me in my affliction....

19 And my God will supply all your needs according to His riches in glory in Christ Jesus.

WRAP IT UP

Psalm 94:19 says, "When my anxious thoughts multiply within me, Your consolations delight my soul." This week you have taken but a sip of the precious life-giving water of God's Word.

As you saw in Jeremiah 17:8, water is essential for life, and our roots need to go deep into the water of His Word. However, sometimes we don't realize just how much we need God, how desperately we need His Word, until life heats up. This was true of the woman at the well who had five husbands and whose thirst wasn't satisfied until Jesus offered her the water of life (John 4).

The refreshing water of God's Word is always available to you. Consider this invitation from the closing verses of the book of Revelation, "The Spirit and the bride say, 'Come.' And let the one who hears say, 'Come.' And let the one who is thirsty come; let the one who wishes take the water of life without cost" (22:17).

The only cost is your time; you choose how you spend it. If you will make time for God, beloved, and get to know Him through His Word, you will experience a peace and power that is literally divine.* And you will be able to live as Paul lived, able to be content in any circumstance and to do all things through Him who strengthens you.

Come, beloved. Drink deeply, for "the people who know their God will display strength and take action" (Daniel 11:32).

---

* For a powerful resource in your efforts to know God better, consider the 40-minute Bible study *The Power of Knowing God.*

We've talked about some of the immediate fears and questions that spring to mind when you find yourself facing divorce. But a change in your marital status can lead to numerous other questions about what your long-term future may hold. How will you deal with the inevitable loneliness? What about sexual temptation? And where does this leave you in relation to God? Can He, will He, ever use you again?

Since we are to live by every word that comes from the mouth of God, let's find out what God says.

OBSERVE

God does not mean for us to go it alone. Friends play a vital role in our spiritual and emotional health, as does the fellowship of a church body. And when you don't have a mate, friends are even more imperative. Let's see what God says in Proverbs, the book of wisdom.

Leader: Read aloud the verses under Selected Proverbs. Have the group...
- *underline every reference to **friend(s).***
- *draw a box around every reference to **counsel, consultation, and counselors.***

SELECTED PROVERBS

17:17 A friend loves at all times, and a brother is born for adversity....

18:24 A man of too many friends comes to ruin, but there is a friend who sticks closer than a brother....

27:6 Faithful are the wounds of a friend, but deceitful are the kisses of an enemy....

9 Oil and perfume make the heart glad, so a man's counsel is sweet to his friend.

10 Do not forsake your own friend or your father's friend....

15:21 Folly is joy to him who lacks sense, but a man of understanding walks straight.

22 Without consultation, plans are frustrated, but with many counselors they succeed.

23 A man has joy in an apt answer, and how delightful is a timely word!

24 The path of life leads upward for the wise that he may keep away from Sheol below.

DISCUSS

• What did you learn from marking the references to friends?

• What purpose(s) do our friends serve? What kind of friends should a person have?

• What did you learn from marking the varied references to counsel and counselors?

OBSERVE

When, as the Bible says, the "arm of flesh" fails (2 Chronicles 32:8), where can you turn?

Leader: Read Psalm 119:22–24 aloud and have the group…
- *mark every **Your** that refers to God with a triangle.*
- *draw a box around every occurrence of **testimonies** and **statutes**.*

DISCUSS

- Describe the circumstances of the psalmist as revealed in these three verses.

- How can you relate to this situation?

- What did the psalmist do? When others failed him, turned against him, did he give up? What can you learn from him?

PSALM 119:22–24

22 Take away reproach and contempt from me, for I observe Your testimonies.

23 Even though princes sit and talk against me, your servant meditates on Your statutes.

24 Your testimonies also are my delight; they are my counselors.

ECCLESIASTES 4:9–12

9 Two are better than one because they have a good return for their labor.

10 For if either of them falls, the one will lift up his companion. But woe to the one who falls when there is not another to lift him up.

11 Furthermore, if two lie down together they keep warm, but how can one be warm alone?

12 And if one can overpower him who is alone, two can resist him. A cord of three strands is not quickly torn apart.

OBSERVE

Leader: Read Ecclesiastes 4:9–12 aloud. Have the group…

- *circle every reference to **two**, including **they, either of them.***
- *underline every reference to **one, who is alone.***

DISCUSS

- What did you learn from marking *two* and *one*?

- What do you believe is the meaning behind the description of the three-strand cord? Who or what might be represented by the third strand?

- Based on what you've read here, why are friends important? And what kind of people do you think they need to be?

- Do you think you should be close friends with a married person of the opposite sex? Explain your answer.

• From what you know of human nature, why would it be a good policy to have women counsel women and men counsel men?

OBSERVE

Feeling lonely or worthless or unlovable can make us vulnerable. We may be tempted to latch on to anyone who treats us with kindness. When we choose close friends and confidants, it's important to find out what they believe, what they claim as their source of wisdom, where they get their worldview. We want to be sure to seek only advice that is grounded in the precepts of God's Word.

Leader: Read 1 Corinthians 15:33 and 2 Corinthians 6:14–18 aloud. Have the group do the following:

• *Underline every **warning** and every **instruction**.*

• *Put a slash like this ╱ between each **contrast** as shown in the first contrast in verse 14.*

1 CORINTHIANS 15:33

Do not be deceived: "Bad company corrupts good morals."

2 CORINTHIANS 6:14–18

14 Do not be bound together with unbelievers; for what partnership have righteousness ╱ and lawlessness, or what fellowship has light with darkness?

15 Or what harmony has Christ with Belial, or what has a believer in common with an unbeliever?

16 Or what agreement has the temple of God with idols? For we are the temple of the living God; just as God said, "I will dwell in them and walk among them; and I will be their God, and they shall be My people.

17 "Therefore, come out from their midst and be separate," says the Lord. "and do not touch what is unclean; and I will welcome you.

18 "And I will be a father to you, and you shall be sons and daughters to Me," says the Lord Almighty.

• *Mark with a cross every reference to **the believer**, including pronouns and synonyms such as **temple of God**.*

DISCUSS
• What instructions did you find in these verses, and what is the reason for each one, if a reason is given? Discuss them carefully, thoughtfully.

• What did you learn from marking the references to the believer?

• What does God promise? Could it be enough if you are so very lonely? How?

• If you are lonely and in need of a godly friend, what are some actions you could take to resolve that loneliness?

OBSERVE

Would it help to talk to the Lord about your need for a friend who meets God's qualifications?

Leader: Read Matthew 7:7–8, 11 aloud and have the group...

- *put a cross over every **you** and the phrase **those who ask.***
- *mark **your Father** and **Him** with a triangle.*

DISCUSS

- What did you learn from marking each *you* and *those who ask?*

- What did you learn from marking *your Father?*

- What does this tell you about the importance of your relationship with God? How should this guide your actions?

MATTHEW 7:7–8, 11

7 Ask, and it will be given to you; seek, and you will find; knock, and it will be opened to you.

8 For everyone who asks receives, and he who seeks finds, and to him who knocks it will be opened....

11 If you then, being evil, know how to give good gifts to your children, how much more will your Father who is in heaven give what is good to those who ask Him!

1 THESSALONIANS 4:3–8

3 For this is the will of God, your sanctification; that is, that you abstain from sexual immorality;

4 that each of you know how to possess his own vessel in sanctification and honor,

5 not in lustful passion, like the Gentiles who do not know God;

6 and that no man transgress and defraud his brother in the matter because the Lord is the avenger in all these things, just as we also told you before and solemnly warned you.

7 For God has not called us for the pur-

OBSERVE

God is very aware of the hormones we have to deal with, the sexual thoughts programmed into our minds. After all, He designed us male and female. He is the creator, the inventor of sex. He intended it to be a pleasurable and healthy activity within the confines of marriage.

As the creator, God also knows the destructive dangers of sex when we don't follow the manufacturer's directions. Therefore He gave us parameters, rules, laws regarding our sexuality. He not only told us the consequences of violating these rules, He also offered His Spirit to give us the power we need to obey.

With this in mind, let's look now at a passage that answers the question of sex outside of marriage.

Leader: Read 1 Thessalonians 4:3–8 aloud slowly. Have the group...

- *underline every reference to the believer—you, your, his, no man, us, he.*

- *put a triangle over every reference to God, including the Lord and pronouns.*

INSIGHT

The word *sanctification* carries with it the concept of holiness, being set apart for God, consecrated to Him. This is the basis of Paul's challenge to believers in this passage.

pose of impurity, but in sanctification.

8 So, he who rejects this is not rejecting man but the God who gives His Holy Spirit to you.

DISCUSS

• What is the main point in these verses? Look at the phrases directed to *you* and *your sanctification*. What is God saying? According to verse 3, what does that sanctification look like? What does it call for?

• What did you learn from marking the references to God, to the Lord?

• According to this passage, what is God's view of sex outside of marriage? Are there any contingency clauses? Exceptions? Special dispensations for divorced people? Explain your answer.

• If you don't believe and obey this, who are you going against?

HEBREWS 13:4
Marriage is to be held in honor among all, and the marriage bed is to be undefiled; for fornicators and adulterers God will judge.

OBSERVE

Leader: *Read Hebrews 13:4 aloud and have the group...*

• *mark every reference to* **marriage** *with two joined circles, like this:* ⭕

• *put a big* **X** *over the phrase* **fornicators and adulterers.**

DISCUSS

• What do you think it means to hold marriage in honor? What is an undefiled marriage bed?

• Who is to hold marriage in honor and keep the bed undefiled?

• Basically, fornication is any kind of sexual activity forbidden in the Bible, while adultery is the infidelity of a person who is married to another. What will happen to those who engage in either of these sins?

• What parallel do you see between Hebrews 13:4 and what you just observed in 1 Thessalonians 4:3–8?

• So what will be your response when someone to whom you're not married wants to become intimate sexually?

OBSERVE

Some turn to pornography to meet their sexual desires. Let's see what Jesus says about this.

Leader: Read Matthew 5:27–30 aloud and have the group...
> • *underline every **you**, **your**, and **his**.*
> • *mark each reference to **hell** with flames, like this:* ⋀⋂⋀

DISCUSS

• What constitutes adultery in this passage? Where is it committed in this case? Note that the Greek word translated here as "looks" is in the present tense, indicating habitual action.

• According to Jesus, how serious is this? What do His comments about the eye and the hand suggest?

MATTHEW 5:27–30

27 You have heard that it was said, "You shall not commit adultery";

28 but I say to you that everyone who looks at a woman with lust for her has already committed adultery with her in his heart.

29 If your right eye makes you stumble, tear it out and throw it from you; for it is better for you to lose one of the parts of your body, than for your whole body to be thrown into hell.

30 If your right hand makes you stumble, cut it off and throw it from you; for it is better for you to lose one of the parts of your body, than for your whole body to go into hell.

• What are the consequences of disobedience in this area?

• According to what you learned earlier about the indwelling Spirit of God, is it possible to resist sexual temptation? Explain your answer.

• In the light of God's Word, is pornography permissible? How does this passage answer the question?

2 TIMOTHY 2:19, 22

19 Nevertheless, the firm foundation of God stands, having this seal, "The Lord knows those who are His," and, "Everyone who names the name of the Lord is to abstain from wickedness."...

OBSERVE

So how can we program our minds? Let's look at one answer that will work if it's obeyed.

Leader: Read aloud 2 Timothy 2:19, 22 and Romans 6:12–14, 19.

   *• Have the group underline **every instruction to those who want to honor God.***

DISCUSS

• What are God's instructions?

• What would obeying these instructions look like in a person's life? How would they be lived out, put into practice? Get specific.

• Do you think it is possible for a person to live this way? Why or why not?

• Is there any excuse for disobedience if you are a child of God? Explain your answer.

• When Paul says "sin shall not be master over you" in Romans 6:14, to whom is he speaking? What does this mean?

• How can you, as a child of God, stop being immoral, resist the pull of pornography, stop doing anything wrong?

22 Now flee from youthful lusts and pursue righteousness, faith, love and peace, with those who call on the Lord from a pure heart.

ROMANS 6:12–14, 19

12 Therefore do not let sin reign in your mortal body so that you obey its lusts,

13 and do not go on presenting the members of your body to sin as instruments of unrighteousness; but present yourselves to God as those alive from the dead, and your members as instruments of righteousness to God.

14 For sin shall not be master over you, for

you are not under law but under grace....

19 I am speaking in human terms because of the weakness of your flesh. For just as you presented your members as slaves to impurity and to lawlessness, resulting in further lawlessness, so now present your members as slaves to righteousness, resulting in sanctification.

ROMANS 8:28–34

28 And we know that God causes all things to work together for good to those who love God, to those who are called according to His purpose.

• What is your responsibility as a child of God? Is His grace sufficient to take you through this? Can choosing to walk in the Spirit really keep you from doing what your flesh wants you to? What did you learn in the earlier weeks of this study?

• What do the verses in 2 Timothy confirm about the importance of the people you hang around, associate with?

Leader: *Have the group discuss the bottom line: Is a divorced, unmarried person to engage in any form of sexual activity?**

OBSERVE

As you consider your new reality, at times you may wonder if your life has been so ruined by divorce that even God has given up on you. Whenever you don't know what to do, what to believe, you need to go to the Sovereign Ruler of the universe. Ask Him to lead you to His Word and to open your

---

* For an in-depth look at this subject, see the 40-minute Bible study *What Does the Bible Say About Sex?*

mind to understand the Scriptures (Luke 24:45). Remember, your Father delights to hear and answer your prayers when they are within the standards of His precepts.

These next verses are among the most healing, comforting, reassuring verses in all the New Testament. And although we looked at a portion of them in an earlier lesson in a different context, let's review them again and then move on to the glorious end of Romans 8. Review helps truth stick better!

Leader: *Read Romans 8:28–34 aloud.*

• *Have the group underline every occurrence of* **those, these, us, elect.**

DISCUSS

• Verse by verse, discuss what you learned from marking these references. What did you learn about the individuals involved? To whom, exactly, do those terms—*those, these, us, elect*—refer?

• What action is taking place in verse 28, and who is behind it?

29 For those whom He foreknew, He also predestined to become conformed to the image of His Son, so that He would be the firstborn among many brethren;

30 and these whom He predestined, He also called; and these whom He called, He also justified; and these whom He justified, He also glorified.

31 What then shall we say to these things? If God is for us, who is against us?

32 He who did not spare His own Son, but delivered Him over for us all, how will He not also with Him freely give us all things?

33 Who will bring a charge against God's elect? God is the one who justifies;

34 who is the one who condemns? Christ Jesus is He who died, yes, rather who was raised, who is at the right hand of God, who also intercedes for us.

• Does this passage say that all things are good? Explain your answer.

• Does being divorced disqualify you from God's promise? Why or why not?

• Would these truths change if you were responsible for the divorce?

• What practical difference would knowing and embracing these truths make for your life? Be specific.

• What did you learn from verse 34 about Jesus in respect to you? Will you believe that and live in the peace of this knowledge?

• Is it possible for God to use your divorce for a redemptive purpose? If you believed that, what difference would it make in your life?

OBSERVE

Leader: Read Romans 8:35–39 aloud. Have the group...

- *underline every **us, we.***
- *draw a heart over **love** and **loved.***

DISCUSS

- What did you learn from marking *us* and *we?* Does this pertain even to a person who has experienced divorce?

- Based on what you read in these verses, do you think divorce can separate you from the love of God in Jesus Christ? In what way might divorce impact your experience of His love?

35 Who will separate us from the love of Christ? Will tribulation, or distress, or persecution, or famine, or nakedness, or peril, or sword?

36 Just as it is written, "For your sake we are being put to death all day long; we were considered as sheep to be slaughtered."

37 But in all these things we overwhelmingly conquer through Him who loved us.

38 For I am convinced that neither death, nor life, nor angels, nor principalities, nor things present, nor things to come, nor powers,

39 nor height, nor depth, nor any other created thing, will be able to separate us from the love of God, which is in Christ Jesus our Lord.

• In light of this truth, beloved of God, how are you going to live?

EPHESIANS 1:3–5

3 Blessed be the God and Father of our Lord Jesus Christ, who has blessed us with every spiritual blessing in the heavenly places in Christ,

4 just as He chose us in Him before the foundation of the world, that we would be holy and blameless before Him. In love

5 He predestined us to adoption as sons through Jesus Christ to Himself, according

OBSERVE

Let's look at two more passages that will assure you that God is not finished with you just because you are divorced.

Leader: Read Ephesians 1:3–5 and Philippians 1:6 aloud.

• *Have the group underline every **us, we, you.***

DISCUSS

• What did you learn from underlining the references to us, the children of God?

• Who is behind our salvation? Who started it? Who will perfect, finish it?

to the kind intention of His will.

For I am confident of this very thing, that He who began a good work in you will perfect it until the day of Christ Jesus.

• If you are a child of God, will divorce, even if it results from your own actions, cut you off from these promises? Give the reason for your answer.

WRAP IT UP

You've seen for yourself God's commandments and His promises. The question now becomes, what will you do with all you've learned? And what will you do when other troublesome questions arise in relation to your divorce?

The Word of God, beloved, has in principle, in precept the answer to every question and situation of life. God says in 2 Peter 1:2–3 that God has given you everything that pertains to life and godliness. Second Timothy 3:16–17 tells us that the Bible, in its whole counsel, is inspired of God—God-breathed.

And it is profitable for teaching. It is, as Jesus said in John 17:17, truth. Truth that can reprove you. It can show you where you are wrong, where you've gone off track, and then correct you, putting you back on that straight and narrow that leads to eternal life (Matthew 7:14). God's Word is also all you need for training in righteousness, to show you what is right and what is wrong.

You get life right when you live according to God's precepts—His standards, not man's!

Has the demise of your marriage left you feeling like damaged goods?

Are you plagued by guilt because of your role in the divorce?

Have you been made to feel "less than" simply because you are divorced?

Are you embarrassed for others to find out that you've been divorced more than once?

Do you wonder if there's any possibility you can get married again?

Don't let your expectations of life be shaped or limited by people who have all sorts of feelings, opinions, and advice but who don't know what God says. Don't be confused or misled by people who don't handle His Word accurately and consequently say and do things they shouldn't.

Once you see for yourself what God says about marriage and divorce, sin and guilt, His truth will set you free. His Word is your life, the bread by which you live (John 17:17; Deuteronomy 32:47; Matthew 4:4). The knowledge of God's truth sanctifies you, sets you apart, and gives you the confidence and strength to move through all sorts of adversity, including the scorn or rejection of others.

In our final week together, let's be sure you have the truth you need for finding hope after divorce.

OBSERVE

Let's begin by looking at the creation of woman, and the first union of man and woman. Then we'll look at the precepts, the truths, that undergird God's design for marriage.

GENESIS 2:18, 21–24

18 Then the LORD God said, "It is not good for the man to be alone; I will make him a helper suitable for him."…

21 So the LORD God caused a deep sleep to fall upon the man, and he slept; then He took one of his ribs and closed up the flesh at that place.

22 The LORD God fashioned into a woman the rib which He had taken from the man, and brought her to the man.

23 The man said, "This is now bone of my bones, and flesh of my flesh; she shall be called Woman,

Leader: *Have the group read aloud Genesis 2:18, 21–24 and Ecclesiastes 9:9. Then read it again and have the group say aloud the key words and mark each as directed.*

- *Mark every reference to **the Lord God,** and every pronoun that refers to Him, with a triangle.*
- *Draw a box around every reference to **the man,** including the pronoun **you** in Ecclesiastes.*
- *Circle all the references to **the woman.***

DISCUSS

- What did you learn from marking the references to the man?

- Describe the connection between the woman and the man. How tight is this relationship, according to verses 23 and 24?

• What is God's role in all that you have just read in Genesis 2?

• What did you learn from Ecclesiastes about marriage—and how does it relate to what you saw in Genesis 2?

• Summarize the bottom line of what you've just read: What is God's perspective on marriage?

• If in marriage two become one, what happens to the one when it is divided by divorce? When you divide the number one what do you get?

because she was taken out of Man."

24 For this reason a man shall leave his father and his mother, and be joined to his wife; and they shall become one flesh.

ECCLESIASTES 9:9

Enjoy life with the woman whom you love all the days of your fleeting life which He has given to you under the sun; for this is your reward in life and in your toil in which you have labored under the sun.

1 CORINTHIANS 6:15–16

15 Do you not know that your bodies are members of Christ? Shall I then take away the members of Christ and make them members of a prostitute? May it never be!

16 Or do you not know that the one who joins himself to a prostitute is one body with her? For He says, "The two shall become one flesh."

OBSERVE

When Genesis 2:24 says that the man and woman would become one flesh, what does that mean? Let's let scripture interpret scripture.

Leader: Read 1 Corinthians 6:15–16.

• *Have the group draw two joined circles over every reference to **body** and **members** (parts of the body), like this:* ⊚

DISCUSS

• According to what you just read in 1 Corinthians, what does "two shall become one flesh" refer to?

• What, if anything, does this understanding of one flesh tell you about the gravity of having sexual intercourse with another person?

• When you have sex with someone, what connection results? What do you become with that person? And if you are married, what does it do to your oneness to bring a third person into the relationship through adultery?

OBSERVE

Let's go to the book of Ephesians, where Genesis 2:24 is quoted again.

Leader: Read Ephesians 5:28–33 and have the group do the following:

• *Put a box around every reference to* **husband(s),** *including synonyms and pronouns.*
• *Circle ever reference to* **wife** *and* **wives,** *including pronouns.*
• *Mark all references to* **Christ,** *including pronouns, with a cross.*

DISCUSS

• What did you learn about the role of the man in respect to his wife?

EPHESIANS 5:28–33

28 So husbands ought also to love their own wives as their own bodies. He who loves his own wife loves himself;

29 for no one ever hated his own flesh, but nourishes and cherishes it, just as Christ also does the church,

30 because we are members of His body.

31 For this reason a man shall leave his

father and mother and shall be joined to his wife, and the two shall become one flesh.

32 This mystery is great; but I am speaking with reference to Christ and the church.

33 Nevertheless, each individual among you also is to love his own wife even as himself, and the wife must see to it that she respects her husband.

- Why is the man to do this? Look at verses 30 and 32.

- What is the wife instructed to do?

- What is marriage a picture of?

- Does divorce fit into that picture? Why or why not?

OBSERVE

As you saw, God wants a man to love his wife as Jesus loves the church. Ecclesiastes says he is to enjoy his wife *all* the days of his life. But divorce, of course, brings an end to this love and enjoyment. So whether your mate has left you or you have left your mate, what does Jesus have to say about your situation? Are you forced to remain single for the rest of your life? We will see. Just remember, redemption is God's mission, so hang in there with me if you grow uncomfortable with what you're reading.

Leader: *Read Matthew 19:3–9 and have the group do the following:*
- *Put a cross over every reference to **Jesus**, including the pronouns **He** and **Him**.*
- *Mark **divorce** with a big **D**.*
- *Put a cloud around the phrase **except for immorality**.*

DISCUSS

- How did this discussion start, and who was it between?

MATTHEW 19:3–9

3 Some Pharisees came to Jesus, testing Him and asking, "Is it lawful for a man to divorce his wife for any reason at all?"

4 And He answered and said, "Have you not read that He who created them from the beginning made them male and female,

5 and said, 'For this reason a man shall leave his father and mother and be joined to his wife, and the two shall become one flesh'?

6 "So they are no longer two, but one flesh. What therefore God has joined together, let no man separate."

⁷ They said to Him, "Why then did Moses command to give her a certificate of divorce and send her away?"

⁸ He said to them, "Because of your hardness of heart Moses permitted you to divorce your wives; but from the beginning it has not been this way.

⁹ "And I say to you, whoever divorces his wife, except for immorality, and marries another woman commits adultery."

- How did Jesus (the Word of God) respond to the question posed in verse 3? To what passage in Scripture did He first point the Pharisees?

- What did you learn from marking *divorce*?

- According to Jesus, is there a valid reason for divorce and thus remarriage? If so, what is it?

- How does forbidding divorce support God's teaching that in marriage two become one flesh in the act of sexual intercourse?

- Although divorce is permissible in the case of immorality, in the light of all you've learned these past six weeks, what would be the ideal even if a mate is unfaithful?

- If immorality was the issue, what would the offended person have to do to help preserve the ideal?

• When a person forgives, whose example do they follow?

• And if the ideal does not happen, is life over? Explain your answer.

OBSERVE

As the Pharisees noted, divorce has been a reality since at least the time of Moses. Let's look at the passage mentioned by Jesus and the religious leaders.

Leader: *Read Deuteronomy 24:1–4. Have the group...*

• *put a box around the references to **the man, the husband**. Number each of these boxed references either 1 or 2 to distinguish between each husband.*

• *circle every reference to **the wife**, including the pronouns **she** and **her**.*

• *mark **divorce** with a big* **D**.

DEUTERONOMY 24:1–4

1 When a man takes a wife and marries her, and it happens that she finds no favor in his eyes because he has found some indecency in her, and he writes her a certificate of divorce and puts it in her hand and sends her out from his house,

2 and she leaves his house and goes and becomes another man's wife,

3 and if the latter husband turns against her and writes her a certificate of divorce and puts it in her hand and sends her out of his house, or if the latter husband dies who took her to be his wife,

4 then her former husband who sent her away is not allowed to take her again to be his wife, since she has been defiled; for that is an abomination before the LORD, and you shall not bring sin on the land which the LORD your God gives you as an inheritance.

INSIGHT

In biblical times, the certificate of divorce was a protection for the woman. It served as proof that her husband had divorced her and thus she was free to remarry.

DISCUSS

• Let's review. What is cited as a reason for divorce in Deuteronomy?

• What are acceptable grounds for divorce, according to Jesus?

• What reason has the first husband given for divorce here in Deuteronomy? (Don't forget what Jesus said about the hardness of heart that led to this.)

INSIGHT

In the culture of Jesus' day, the definition of "some indecency in her" was stretched to cover anything the man didn't like about the woman and became an excuse for his hardness of heart toward his wife.

• Review the situation: How many times is the woman in this passage married? How many certificates of divorce are given to her?

• In the context of all you've learned so far, what did the certificate permit the woman to do?

• According to these verses, can a person remarry their first mate after marrying another? What if mate number two dies? Why do you think it is this way? (Remember all you learned about "one flesh" in Genesis 2:24.)

MALACHI 2:13–16

13 "This is another thing you do: you cover the altar of the LORD with tears, with weeping and with groaning, because He no longer regards the offering or accepts it with favor from your hand.

14 "Yet you say, 'For what reason?' Because the LORD has been a witness between you and the wife of your youth, against whom you have dealt treacherously, though she is your companion and your wife by covenant.

15 "But not one has done so who has a remnant of the Spirit. And what did that one do while he was seeking a godly offspring?

OBSERVE

Malachi, the last book of the Old Testament, is directed toward people of Israel, including the priests, who are not honoring God as they should. Consequently, God cannot honor them. In this passage God points out one of the things that causes Him to withhold His favor.

Leader: *Read Malachi 2:13–16. Have the group say aloud and...*

- *underline every reference to **the wife,** including pronouns.*
- *mark **divorce** with a big* **D.**
- *mark **treacherously** with a big* **T.**

DISCUSS

- What was the situation here? Look at where you marked the references to the wife. What do you learn?

- What was the Lord's perspective on this? What did He accuse the man of doing?

• What did you learn from marking *divorce*?

INSIGHT

Malachi 2:16 is very difficult to translate from the Hebrew. The English Standard Version translates the verse this way: "For the man who does not love his wife but divorces her, says the Lord, the God of Israel, covers his garment with violence, says the Lord of hosts. So guard yourselves in your spirit, and do not be faithless."

Take heed then to your spirit, and let no one deal treacherously against the wife of your youth.

16 "For I hate divorce," says the LORD, the God of Israel, "and him who covers his garment with wrong," says the LORD of hosts. "So take heed to your spirit, that you do not deal treacherously."

• Read verse 15. What do you see here regarding the potential impact of divorce on the children, the offspring of the marriage?

1 CORINTHIANS 7:1–3, 5

¹ Now concerning the things about which you wrote, it is good for a man not to touch a woman.

² But because of immoralities, each man is to have his own wife, and each woman is to have her own husband.

³ The husband must fulfill his duty to his wife, and likewise also the wife to her husband....

⁵ Stop depriving one another, except by agreement for a time, so that you may devote yourselves to prayer, and come together again so that Satan will

OBSERVE

Let's look at Paul's letter to the Corinthians and see what insights we can glean from his words to those living in a culture similar to ours—a culture of rampant immorality. These new Christians wanted to know what they should do in respect to sex and marriage now that they belonged to Christ. "What about sex? What if I'm married to someone who is not a believer? How do I live with her or him? If I am divorced, can I marry again? Should I go back to my unsaved mate? Should a virgin even get married?" Paul (who was unmarried) answered those questions and more in 1 Corinthians 7. It is a critical chapter.

We will begin with what Paul says about sex in marriage and then consider what he says to those who are married, unmarried, and divorced.

Leader: Read 1 Corinthians 7: 1–3, 5 aloud and have the group...

- *put a box around every reference to **the man, the husband**.*
- *circle every reference to **the wife, the woman**.*

DISCUSS

• What is the issue in these verses? Look at the context.

• What does it mean for the husband and the wife to fulfill their duty to one another? And if they don't, what is the potential problem?

• So can Christians have sex? If so, under what circumstances?

OBSERVE

Leader: Read 1 Corinthians 7:8–11 aloud and have the group do the following:

• *Draw a wavy line under every reference to **the unmarried** and **widows**, include pronouns, like this:* ‿‿‿‿

• *Draw a box around every reference to **the husband**, including pronouns.*

• *Circle every reference to **the wife**, including pronouns.*

• *Mark **leave** with a big **L**.*

• *Mark **divorce** with a big **D**.*

1 CORINTHIANS 7:8–11

not tempt you because of your lack of self-control.

8 But I say to the unmarried and to widows that it is good for them if they remain even as I.

9 But if they do not have self-control, let them marry; for it is better to marry than to burn with passion.

10 But to the married I give instructions, not I, but the Lord, that the wife should not leave her husband

11 (but if she does leave, she must remain unmarried, or else be reconciled to her husband), and that the husband should not divorce his wife.

DISCUSS

• What are God's instructions through Paul to the unmarried? What reasons did Paul give?

• What did you learn from verse 9 and the reference to self-control? What does this tell you about sex outside of marriage?

• What are the Lord's instructions to wives and husbands in verses 10–11?

• Does verse 11 allow for remarriage? Explain your answer.

1 CORINTHIANS 7:12–16

12 But to the rest I say, not the Lord, that if any brother has a wife who is an unbeliever, and she consents to live with him, he must not divorce her.

13 And a woman who has an unbeliev-

OBSERVE

Paul now turns specifically to those who are married to unbelievers.

Leader: Read 1 Corinthians 7:12–16 aloud and have the group…

  • *put a box around the references to* **brother, husband,** *including the appropriate pronouns.*

  • *circle the references to* **wife, woman, sister,** *including the appropriate pronouns.*

Leader: Read the text again. This time have the group...
- mark **unbeliever, unbelieving** with a big **XX.**
- mark **divorce, send away,** and **leaves** with a big **D.**

DISCUSS

- What are God's instructions to a believing spouse of an unbeliever who wants to leave the marriage?

- What reason is given for staying with an unbelieving spouse who does not want to leave?

Note: Because this study is focused on finding hope after divorce, the issue of physical abuse is not covered. However, from all God says about marriage, it is obvious that physical abuse is not acceptable, and the abused have a right to remove themselves from such behavior.

ing husband, and he consents to live with her, she must not send her husband away.

14 For the unbelieving husband is sanctified through his wife, and the unbelieving wife is sanctified through her believing husband; for otherwise your children are unclean, but now they are holy.

15 Yet if the unbelieving one leaves, let him leave; the brother or the sister is not under bondage in such cases, but God has called us to peace.

16 For how do you know, O wife, whether you will save

your husband? Or
how do you know,
O husband, whether
you will save your
wife?

INSIGHT

Sanctified means "set apart." First
Corinthians 7:14 is not saying that
an unbeliever will be saved through
marriage, only that he or she will
benefit from the union with a mate
who belongs to God. The presence of
the believing spouse also helps protect the children.

• If the unbeliever leaves, does this free the
believer to eventually marry? Explain your
answer.

INSIGHT

When the Word of God grants
divorce, then it permits remarriage.
When you read "not under bondage"
in 1 Corinthians 7:15, it means the
person in this circumstance is no
longer obligated to the marriage.

OBSERVE

First Corinthians 7 provides guidance about matters of divorce and remarriage for those who are recently saved, called to Jesus Christ. In verses 17–20 Paul noted that we should remain in whatever situation we were in when called. The verses we will look at next explain what this means in regard to marital status.

If you were already divorced before you were saved, you'll find this very helpful. As a newly saved divorcée, I found these verses liberating, especially as some were telling me I could never remarry if I wanted to obey God. (This was before my former husband committed suicide.)

Leader: Read 1 Corinthians 7:26–28 aloud and have the group...

- mark **bound, marry, married** with two joined circles: ⭕⭕
- mark **released** as you marked divorce, with a big **D.**

1 CORINTHIANS 7:26–28

26 I think then that this is good in view of the present distress, that it is good for man to remain as he is.

27 Are you bound to a wife? Do not seek to be released. Are you released from a wife? Do not seek a wife.

28 But if you marry, you have not sinned; and if a virgin marries, she has not sinned. Yet such will have trouble in this life, and I am trying to spare you.

INSIGHT

The term *bound* is synonymous with *married*, and *released* is synonymous with *divorced*.

DISCUSS

• What was Paul's advice to the new believers in regard to their current marital status?

• So if you already were divorced when you became saved, are you allowed to get married? Where's your answer in these verses?

• What did you learn about marriage in these verses? Is it free from trouble? Did you expect it to be?

• How should what you've learned this week guide your decisions concerning remarriage? Should you be in a hurry to get married?

OBSERVE

Many people who are divorced carry a burden of guilt that keeps them from moving on and serving the Lord. What can you do with guilt, especially if you are the one who—right or wrong—caused or asked for the divorce?

Leader: Read 1 John 1:8–9 aloud and have the group...

* *mark every reference to sin and unrighteousness with a big S.*
* *underline every we, us, ourselves.*

1 JOHN 1:8–9

8 If we say that we have no sin, we are deceiving ourselves and the truth is not in us.

9 If we confess our sins, He is faithful and righteous to forgive us our sins and to cleanse us from all unrighteousness.

INSIGHT

The word for "confess" in the Greek is *homologeo,* which means "to say the same thing." In other words *to confess* is to agree with God that what He calls sin, you call the same. It means to name your sin for what it is—adultery, lying, etc.—rather than making excuses or trying to soften the truth.

DISCUSS

• What did you learn from marking *we, us,* and *ourselves?*

• So how is sin to be dealt with?

• What does God do when we deal with sin as He directs? Don't miss a thing God promises to do.

• What should this mean in respect to carrying guilt?

• How many times do you think you have to confess a sin before God will do what He says?

HEBREWS 10:12–18

12 But He, having offered one sacrifice for sins for all time, sat down at the right hand of God,

OBSERVE

Jesus came to this world for the purpose of setting us free from the penalty, the power, and eventually the presence of sin. "The Son of Man has come to seek and to save that which was lost" and to forgive sins (Luke 19:10; Luke 1:76–77).

Let's consider one final Scripture passage that should settle the issue of guilt. We'll look at it in two parts so you can observe it well and then embrace the truth in faith's obedience.

Leader: *Read Hebrews 10:12–18 aloud. Have the group do the following:*

- *Put a cross over every pronoun referring to **Jesus**—every **He, His.***
- *Underline every reference to **those who are sanctified**, including the pronouns.*
- *Put a big **S** over every reference to **sin**, including **lawless deeds.***

INSIGHT

Hebrews 10:14 says that the offering of Jesus, the shedding of His blood for our sins, "has perfected for all time those who are sanctified." The phrasing here is in the present tense in the Greek, which means it is a continual process. In other words, we keep getting set apart more and become more like Jesus! Awesome, isn't it?

¹³ waiting from that time onward until His enemies be made a footstool for His feet.

¹⁴ For by one offering He has perfected for all time those who are sanctified.

¹⁵ And the Holy Spirit also testifies to us; for after saying,

¹⁶ "This is the covenant that I will make with them after those days, says the Lord: I will put My laws upon their heart, and on their mind I will write them," He then says,

¹⁷ "And their sins and their lawless deeds I will remember no more."

18 Now where there is forgiveness of these things, there is no longer any offering for sin.

DISCUSS

• Look at each place you marked a reference to Jesus. What has God done for you in and through Jesus? And how did He do it?

• Is there anything you can do, or are told to do, to pay for your sin?

• How is sin taken care of? For how long?

HEBREWS 10:19–23

19 Therefore, brethren, since we have confidence to enter the holy place by the blood of Jesus,

20 by a new and living way which He inaugurated for us

OBSERVE

Leader: Read Hebrews 10:19–23. Have the group do the following:

• *Underline every reference to* **believers,** *including* **brethren, we, us, our.**

• *Put a cross over every reference to* **Jesus,** *including* **great priest** *and the appropriate pronouns.*

• *Put a box around* **evil conscience.**

• *Mark* **hope** *with a big* **H.**

DISCUSS

• What did you learn from marking the references to believers, the brethren? So what is the application? What is the *therefore* there for in verse 19?

• According to these verses, do your past sins obligate you to walk around burdened by an evil conscience? Why or why not?

• What is God's answer for our guilt?

through the veil, that is, His flesh,

21 and since we have a great priest over the house of God,

22 let us draw near with a sincere heart in full assurance of faith, having our hearts sprinkled clean from an evil conscience and our bodies washed with pure water.

23 Let us hold fast the confession of our hope without wavering, for He who promised is faithful.

WRAP IT UP

A precious friend, who loves Jesus dearly, told me that for five years she carried the guilt of her divorce, asking God over and over again to forgive her. Then one day she fell to her knees and said, "God, You know how sorry I am. You know my heart. You know I love You and I want to be right with You. I cannot carry the weight of this guilt anymore, and I am not getting up from here until You lift its burden."

Then God said, *I have forgiven you. Believe Me. Accept My forgiveness.* The Lord then brought Psalm 51 to her mind. With that, she said, her burden of guilt was lifted—and has never returned.

Jesus paid for your sins in full, beloved of God, once for all, forever. Isn't it presumptuous on your part to think you can add to Jesus' sacrifice in order to get forgiveness of sin and freedom from guilt when God said there remains no more sacrifice for sin (Hebrews 10:12)? His sacrifice took care of all our sins, past, present, and future—believe Him. Thank Him. Show your gratitude by living in the light of that truth, whether or not others believe it. Forgetting those things which are behind, press on to the prize of the high calling of Jesus Christ (Philippians 3:14). Make your life count.

I urge you to read Luke 7:36–50, where you'll find the account of a woman whose sins were many, and because she knew how much she was forgiven, she loved Jesus even more. It was to that woman, disdained by the religious establishment of her day, that Jesus said, "Your faith has saved you; go in peace" (verse 50).

May you, beloved, go in peace—the peace and power that come from faith, from taking God at His Word.